Akathist to Father John

his akathist is for private use as Father John is not canoı.

Kontakion 1

'ome, lovers of the faithful, let us praise together the Most Reverend Father John of Colciu, who as shown himself to be an icon of bloodless sacrifice and a bearer of the philokalic life, singing to im and saying in one voice: Rejoice, Father John, branch of Athos, beloved of the faithful!

Ekos 1

enerable Father John, you said that "he who puts his hand to the plough and turns back does not ter the kingdom of God". Having been a shepherd since your youth, you walked to the end of ur life on the narrow path to which Christ called you, and for this we give you these praises:

ejoice, for in a faithful and virtuous family you have grown up;

ejoice, that Saint George has helped you, receiving his name in baptism;

ejoice, for you sought bloodless martyrdom and laboured much;

ejoice, that your parents have had the blessing to host the Athonite monks;

ejoice, that for their toil your father and your mother were rewarded by Christ;

ejoice, that from your youth you have known monks enriched in virtues;

ejoice, that you chose to follow them in faith and piety;

ejoice, that you have put your love of God above that of your parents;

ejoice, that you have brought the thought of your repentance to fulfilment;

ejoice, lover of solitude, that you have gone to peace;

ejoice, for praying to the Mother of God in her garden;

ejoice, Father John, branch of Athos, beloved of the faithful!

Kontakion 2

As you boarded the ship to the Holy Mountain, you were covered by a monk with his robe, so that you would not be seen, but you were also covered by the Blessed Mother of God with her holy covering, so that, living in her garden, you might bring praise to the Lord: Alleluia!

Ekos 2

Your father tried hard to persuade you to return from Colciu Hermitage, but, seeing that you did not bow to his pleas, he asked you: "See to it that you die here". And you obeyed his advice and took your vows in the Holy Mountain of Athos, following in the footsteps of the saints of old, and for this we praise you, saying:

Rejoice, for the saints of the Athos guided you;

Rejoice, that in their unseen prayers they have sustained you;

Rejoice, that through prayer you have found God in your heart;

Rejoice, the Mother of God has covered you unceasingly;

Rejoice, that she has guided your steps to the Chapel of Saint John the Baptist;

Rejoice, that the Almighty has given you strength on the narrow path of your trials;

Rejoice, that Christ has been sanctified in your heart and enlightened you with His grace;

Rejoice, that you did not hear your father's plea to leave the Holy Mountain;

Rejoice, that the Lord has turned your father's heart and made a gift to the hermitage;

Rejoice, that you have been your father's tutor to holiness through patience and steadfastness;

Rejoice, who teaches us to forsake our own will;

Rejoice, Father John, branch of Athos, beloved of the faithful!

Kontakion 3

"Father John was a mystery. Of all the monks I have known or met, he fulfilled what the Church tells us more than anyone else today", testified the Most Reverend Father Dionysius the Blind of Colciu, who before your passing to the Lord confessed you for the last time, and marvelling at your humility and your neediness, sang to God: Alleluia!

Ekos 3

Forgive me, Lord, for I have not yet become a monk", you prayed at the end of your earthly life, being a lesson of true humility and urging us to leave pride and self-esteem. And we, being rebuked by your humility, honour you by saying:

Rejoice, good aroma of humility and modesty;

Rejoice, you who taught us that without God's help we can do no good;

Rejoice, that the benevolent Father Elias was your first priest and confessor;

Rejoice, that you have striven to obey in all things;

Rejoice, that in the fire of temptation by the loosing of your will you were kept from falling;

Rejoice, lover of virginity, that you have sought the parables of the divine life;

Rejoice, that in finding them you have followed them through your devotion;

Rejoice, that together with Father Dionysius you praised Christ;

Rejoice, that the Lord has blessed your spiritual bond;

Rejoice, that in your time many saints in the Athonite land have also been in repentance;

Rejoice, that you prayed together in spirit and God received you into his kingdom;

Rejoice, Father John, branch of Athos, beloved of the faithful!

Kontakion 4

"If you cannot profit from my silence, then you will not profit from my word," you said to a monk who had come to you for teaching, showing that you were the fruit of the Patristic fathers over the ages, bringing the Lord the silent song through your life: Alleluia!

Ekos 4

You went to pick olives on your knees, with sick limbs, unaware of your sickness and pain, and with the ink of your strong devotions you wrote in the souls of those who saw you a useful parable and for this after your passing to the Lord they brought you songs of praise:

Rejoice, that you followed the fidelity of Saint Anthony the Great;

Rejoice, that you have cast off all worldly cares;

Rejoice, you who have kept the habit of silence and self-denial;

Rejoice, teacher of detachment from the world and of alienation;

Rejoice, you who at the Holy Places are filled with heavenly blessing;

Rejoice, that in the unseen feast of Pascha the divine light covered you;

Rejoice, you who on the Calvary of suffering climbed steadfastly;

Rejoice, you who by the prayer of your heart burned unceasingly;

Rejoice, that with prayers and psalms in your heart you have built an altar to the Lord;

Rejoice, protector of monks and patron of pilgrims;

Rejoice, worthy heir of the graces of your abbots;

Rejoice, Father John, branch of Athos, beloved of the faithful!

Kontakion 5

Your words reaching us, that "only he who endures knows how to love", have gained strength by feeding us with them. For you, bearing your cross without quarrels and enduring the attacks of the devilish forces without being troubled, have brought to the Lord the song: Alleluia!

Ekos 5

Be patient, but with joy, not with soul-punishment and carping," you told a monk, and your words brought light to his soul. We delight to follow your teachings as if we had heard them in our own ears and for this we praise you, saying:

Rejoice, for from your youth you have been a lover of peace;

Rejoice, that you have been steadfast in faithfulness and obedience;

Rejoice, that from God you have received power against the devil;

Rejoice, that you have fought the fallen angels through the watchfulness;

Rejoice, that you cast out the devils who tempt those who honour you;

Rejoice, the example of your labours is used by many monks;

Rejoice, you have taught the young monks by your patience;

Rejoice, for you have forgiven them and shown them the remedy of repentance;

Rejoice, that you call the prodigals to the way of faith;

Rejoice, you change the hearts of those overcome by impatience;

Rejoice, for your grace you have received heavenly reward;

Rejoice, Father John, branch of Athos, beloved of the faithful!

Kontakion 6

You lived covered by the grace of the saints who were in penance at the Colciu Hermitage, learning from Saint Agapius the way of the martyrdom of obedience and from the martyrs killed by the Turks the way of suffering without charity, and increasing your penance you taught us to sing to God: Alleluia!

Ekos 6

Saint Paisie the Aghiorite testified that due to the increase of sin many saints of the old times woul
have liked to live in our times, to be in struggle. But, more than that, you wished to live in the time
of great upheaval when the Antichrist will come, in order to witness Christ, and we, seeing your
rapacity and courage, say to you:

Rejoice, with the saints of the Garden of the Mother of God;

Rejoice, you resembled the angels in following the hermits;

Rejoice, by grace the Aghiorite son of Saint Athanasius;

Rejoice, son of obedience, disciple of Saint Agapius;

Rejoice, the ravishment of the Colciu fathers has borne fruit in your soul;

Rejoice, that the prayers of the saints of Athos have strengthened you;

Rejoice, you who are a companion to those who bear the cross of affliction;

Rejoice, through many sicknesses and pains you have taken the crown of martyrdom;

Rejoice, you lift up those brought to their knees by the impurity of faith;

Rejoice, banisher of fear and dismay from those overcome by trouble;

Rejoice, you bring comfort to the Christian until the end of time;

Rejoice, Father John, branch of Athos, beloved of the faithful!

Kontakion 7

God made you a fisher of men, for by your parable you called many to monastic devotions, just as
you did with your sister, who received the name of Onuphria in monasticism. Through your few
words God has worked more than through the preaching of others, and for this your disciples
brought the Lord the song: Alleluia!

Ekos 7

ou loved the cross of monastic obedience and lived covered by the grace of blessing, doing

othing according to your will. And when the fathers returned with empty nets, for they had caught

o fish for the feast of the Church of Saint John the Baptist, you, praying in silence, sent them to

ring the great fish. They obeyed without reading and with empty hands caught a large fish near the

1ore, and for this we praise your faith, saying to you:

ejoice, that for your prayers your disciples have seen the fruits of obedience;

ejoice, fisher of souls, that the words of Scripture have come to life;

ejoice, that in the way of need and obedience they followed you;

ejoice, for your sister, widowed, set out for the monastic life;

ejoice, that in the course of her monastic ministry her hearing was restored;

ejoice, her bodily powers were wonderfully strengthened;

ejoice, that Mother Onuphria in piety, in devotion and in humility resembled you;

ejoice, that you call the devout to take up the monastic cross;

ejoice, that you are a protection for those who want to enter the monastery without a call;

ejoice, you are the rock of the monks who in prayer call you with piety;

ejoice, praying for the laymen who bear the cross of the family worthily;

ejoice, Father John, branch of Athos, beloved of the faithful!

Kontakion 8

e have heeded your advice, "Be careful what book you read, for that spirit will be imprinted in

ou," and, seeing in you the icon of holiness and the candle that has burned with the oil of the

achings of the saints of old, we ask you to help us also to cast out soul-killing idleness, to praise

od, saying: Alleluia!

Ekos 8

From the little you saved, you strived to do almsgiving, to help the poor, but you also supported the printing of spiritual teachings, being part of a blessed work of preaching the faith, and the Lord received your sacrifice as He received the money of the widow in the Gospel. For this we joyfully bring you these praises:

Rejoice, for your mercies you have received heavenly payment;

Rejoice, treasure, which the lovers of charity have discovered;

Rejoice, you who have taught that silence is the most useful of words;

Rejoice, book written by the Saviour Christ with the pen of the Holy Spirit;

Rejoice, psalmist, who by your life has sung to God;

Rejoice, gracious son of the Mother of God, who has shown you so much mercy;

Rejoice, Saint John the Baptist has given you his blessing;

Rejoice, that from the teachings of Saint John Jacob you have fed;

Rejoice, for you have gathered like a bee the useful words of the saints;

Rejoice, that by the spiritual books you have adapted yourself from the fountain of the Fathers;

Rejoice, that by the simplicity of your life you have reached the depths of theology;

Rejoice, Father John, branch of Athos, beloved of the faithful!

Kontakion 9

Coming to you the hierarch who wanted you to pray for the quieting of the disturbances made by the Turks and for the peace of the world and asking what he could do for you, you asked him to keep the dogmas of the Sovereign Church unchanged, showing yourself a follower of the holy confessors in zeal for the preservation of the holy teaching, and for this we praise God, singing: Alleluia!

Ekos 9

Having grieved at the abandonment of the ordinances of the fathers of old and the imposition of the spirit of neglect even in the Garden of the Mother of God, you preached by the parable of your life that the goal of life is the acquisition of heaven and that if we lose heaven, we lose everything, and by your silence you preached more than other priests by their skilful words, and for this we praise you:

Rejoice, for you have acquired the heaven;

Rejoice, for you have not lost the heavenly beauty you sought;

Rejoice, for you have opened your soul to the beauty of the holy services;

Rejoice, that now you praise God with the powers of the incorporeal;

Rejoice, for you have exhorted that hierarch to keep the dogmas of the Church undefiled;

Rejoice, that through your voice the voice of the holy confessors has resounded;

Rejoice, that by your counsel you also teach the hierarchs of our time;

Rejoice, rebuking those who defile the boundaries of the faith of the Sovereign Church;

Rejoice, guardian of the teaching of the Holy Fathers;

Rejoice, lover of the teaching and canons of righteousness;

Rejoice, who rejected the soul-damaging renovations;

Rejoice, Father John, branch of Athos, beloved of the faithful!

Kontakion 10

You have endured the misery of sickness like a new Job, for with sick feet you did not leave the needy, but in the furnace of sorrows you cleansed your soul, urging us also, the passionate and lovers of pleasures, to put away worldly desires and to sing to the Lord, Alleluia!

Ekos 10

Seeing how you endured the multitude of sufferings brought on by the diseases with which God tried you, in order to multiply your crowns, the doctors marveled, as an angel in the flesh you showed yourself, loving suffering like the ancient martyrs, and for this we dare to praise you, saying:

Rejoice, holy soul, cleansed in the furnace of suffering;

Rejoice, for you allowed yourself to be crucified on the cross of pain and sickness;

Rejoice, by the grace of the Holy Spirit as a new Job you have endured;

Rejoice, you have left your life in God's hands;

Rejoice, you counted it a blessing to have sickness of lungs and sore feet;

Rejoice, for after your falling asleep God gave you the gift of healing the sick;

Rejoice, that by your patience you are like the saints of old;

Rejoice, that you healed many a sick person who was in great pain;

Rejoice, that you prayed for Christians who were undergoing difficult operations;

Rejoice, seeing the children who came into the world for your prayers;

Rejoice, that knowing of your miracles in faith we are strengthened;

Rejoice, Father John, branch of Athos, beloved of the faithful!

Kontakion 11

Asked what you have acquired in your long life in Holy Mount Athos, you answered with humilit that you have gained boldness before God. Then your disciple asked you to pray that you might have a spring nearer to the monastery, and not long afterwards, when your prayers were answered he sang to the Lord with thanksgiving: Alleluia!

Ekos 11

ince your lifetime the work of your gifts has been evident, chosen vessel of the Holy Spirit, and for is, praying that you may be our protector on the way of salvation, we want to venerate your holy lics and praise you, saying:

ejoice, for often before you were asked you wisely answered;

ejoice, you covered the multitude of your graces with humility;

ejoice, for you have been given the gift of foresight;

ejoice, you foresaw a young monk's ordination;

ejoice, that you have known the spirit of the vatopedian monk's monasticism;

ejoice, that by the parable of your life you have called souls to the monastery;

ejoice, you knew before death you would see your grandson again;

ejoice, for in your presence the unruly young man was softened;

ejoice, in the purity of your soul he listened to you;

ejoice, for you soften the passions of those in the sea of temptation;

ejoice, that in the way of virtue you are the tutor of the monks;

ejoice, Father John, branch of Athos, beloved of the faithful!

Kontakion 12

a wonderful way you showed yourself to the father who had come to bow at your tomb and said him: "Even if I died, you know that I am still alive". And he, understanding that you had cended to the heights of holiness, praised God, who had crowned you, with a voice of joy, nging: Alleluia!

Ekos 12

God gave us testimony of your gifts when your holy relics sprang forth good fragrance and He ordained that they should be distributed in various places, so that the news of your holiness might spread and the faithful might flock to your help. And we, standing before your holy icon as if befo your holy relics, praise you, saying:

Rejoice, for at the burial of your body the sweetness of your mercy was felt;

Rejoice, for at the burial of your holy relics the fragrance was poured forth;

Rejoice, these have reached many places by the mercy of God;

Rejoice, your miracles never cease to multiply;

Rejoice, for the measure of your outpouring of myrrh is seen;

Rejoice, that by your prayers and your sufferings you have sanctified your body;

Rejoice, for you came to the aid of the woman who suffered after the operation;

Rejoice, that by praying at the casket of your holy relics she recovered from depression;

Rejoice that you healed the sick who prayed to you for help;

Rejoice, that the people helped by you have proclaimed your miracles;

Rejoice, for you have shown yourself to be a miracle-worker and patron of our heavenly Father;

Rejoice, Father John, branch of Athos, beloved of the faithful!

Kontakion 13

Most Reverend Father John, praise of Colciu, who shines in the choir of the holy Athonites, who protect the monks who walk in your footsteps, bearing the cross of obedience, prayer, humility and bloodless martyrdom, receive now this little prayer and pray for us, the weak, powerless and sinners, that by changing our lives we may make a good beginning of salvation and sing to the Lo until the end of our lives: Alleluia! (thrice)

Ekos 1

Venerable Father John, you said that "he who puts his hand to the plough and turns back does not enter the kingdom of God". Having been a shepherd since your youth, you walked to the end of your life on the narrow path to which Christ called you, and for this we give you these praises:

Rejoice, for in a faithful and virtuous family you have grown up;

Rejoice, that Saint George has helped you, receiving his name in baptism;

Rejoice, for you sought bloodless martyrdom and laboured much;

Rejoice, that your parents have had the blessing to host the Athonite monks;

Rejoice, that for their toil your father and your mother were rewarded by Christ;

Rejoice, that from your youth you have known monks enriched in virtues;

Rejoice, that you chose to follow them in faith and piety;

Rejoice, that you have put your love of God above that of your parents;

Rejoice, that you have brought the thought of your repentance to fulfilment;

Rejoice, lover of solitude, that you have gone to peace;

Rejoice, for praying to the Mother of God in her garden;

Rejoice, Father John, branch of Athos, beloved of the faithful!

Kontakion 1

Come, lovers of the faithful, let us praise together the Most Reverend Father John of Colciu, who has shown himself to be an icon of bloodless sacrifice and a bearer of the philokalic life, singing to him and saying in one voice: Rejoice, Father John, branch of Athos, beloved of the faithful!

Prayer to Father John

Most Holy Father John, the praise of Colciu Hermitage and the adornment of Holy Mount Athos, receive this little prayer from us who run to you as to a gracious benefactor and helper and who, bowing our hearts, pray to you: see our sorrows, see our bitterness and the temptations through which we pass. Father, hasten to help us with your prayers and sustain us, in this hour and all the days of our lives. Take heed of our sighs and do not overlook us, for weak and helpless we are, but we know, holy one of God, that if you have endured sickness and suffering of every kind, he who has been blessed by you and with faith has prayed to you has not remained helpless. For who, after your passage to the Lord, prayed to you and remained unanswered?

We know that during your life, when you were living in the Garden of the Mother of God, you hastened to come to the aid of those who needed your help, and after your death you multiplied your mercies, showing yourself to be a miracle-worker through the gift you received from Christ. You are for us the living icon of faith, obedience, prayer, devotion and patience. These virtues of yours have also made us believe that you will not deny us our prayers, nor will you cast us away due to our little faith. Our faith is weak, but we have hope in your intercessions, that you will help us too, as you have helped all who have come to you in prayer.

We pray to you, Most Reverend Father John, that you will pray for us to Christ, the Son of God, who has not overlooked your prayers, but has heard and fulfilled them, according to the multitude of His love for mankind.

Therefore, we fall down before your icon with the piety with which we would stand before your holy relics and ask that you would be our protector on the way to salvation. We do not know how to pray nor do we know what to ask for in our prayers. We do not see our shortcomings and sins, being blinded by pride and self-love. But, being sick and afflicted, we do not forsake our salvation but call upon you to come quickly to our help, as you have come every time you have been called in prayer. Help us, holy one, to change our lives, to put our salvation on the right footing. Help us to learn humility, and meekness, help us to walk the path of prayer and love. And with the gift of Christ, who has enlightened you, being strengthened and enlightened, may we offer you songs of praise and honour to the Triune God glorified, Father and Son and Holy Spirit, forever and ever. Amen.

Prayer 2

O' Most Holy Father John, you who have been blessed by the Most Gracious God and have entered into the kingdom of heaven, do not let us, the lowly, the sinful and the unworthy, remain outside like the five foolish virgins, but pray to the Most Merciful God and to His Blessed Mother to grant us the kingdom above. And as you prayed for the woman who was unwilling to bear children, and she received a blessed birth, so pray that we too may receive the gift of tears, repentance and humility, that we may weep unceasingly for our bitter sins. And as you prayed that the water might flow from the spring beside the cell in which you struggled, so help us also, the lowly and unworthy, to thirst always for spiritual water, as the psalmist says: "As the hart desires the springs of water, so my soul desires you, O' Lord". And as you have received from God the gift of love of neighbour, of simplicity and humility, the gift of patience and gentleness, so pray that we too may acquire these virtues, which are necessary for every faithful Christian.

O' Most Holy Father John, who are the light of the Good Lord, who was not put under a bushel, but was set in the candlestick, to give light to all, so enlighten also the dark eyes of our souls, that we may honour your name and unceasingly with you and the angels praise the name of the Most Holy Trinity, always, now and ever and unto ages of ages. Amen.

Prayer on help to salvation

Most Reverend Father John of Colciu, patron of monks and intercessor in prayer for all Christian people, please receive my prayer in this hour of need. Help me and take me under the cover of your prayers, as the Greek monk took you under his rasa, when you got on the ship to go to the Holy Mount Athos. Help me, Most Holy Father, by praying for me, the sinner, that I may know and do the will of God.

Show yourself to me, my swift helper, that I do not desire worldly goodness and pleasure, but the doing of God's will. But my mind is feeble and the ears of my soul are diseased and I do not hear the call of the Lord. The voice of my conscience is mingled with the whispers of the spirit of this world. What shall I do, Father? To whom shall I run? Where shall I find a word of help? I place my hope in the help of the Most Holy Mother of God, patroness of monks and monasteries and of all

Christian families, but I have faith that you will help me too, Father John, to make the right decision.

If it is God's will that I choose the monastic path, help me to find a wise and obedient tutor in which to live. Guide my steps on this path, keeping me from idleness and from falling, keeping me from temptations left and right. Strengthen and increase by your prayers my love for the holy things, that I may walk the narrow way, on which all the holy men of the Church have walked.

If it is God's will that I choose family life, help me not to let it be for my own soul's sake, but for the salvation of myself and those close to me. If salvation in the monastery is hard, how can it be easy in the family, when the spirit of this world has spoiled the ordinances of Christian life, when disunity and sin have struck at the bond bound and blessed by God Himself? Help me, Father, don't leave me.

And if it is God's will that I should remain in the world, bearing the cross of solitude, help me that it may not be to me to perdition or to the imputing of my few needs, but that it may be to me for salvation.

Therefore I ask you, Most Holy Father John, pray for me, the sinner, that I may know and do the will of God, as God directs. You said that "more prayer, more humility and more love of God will easily lead us to the kingdom of heaven". Grant me that through prayer, humility and love of God I too may acquire eternal goodness, glorifying God, the Most High, the Father, the Son and the Holy Spirit for ever and ever. Amen.

Printed in Great Britain
by Amazon

21728734R00020